The Linen Cupboard

The Linen Cupboard

GLORIA NICOL

TEXT BY
GILLIAN HASLAM

Trafalgar Square Publishing

CONTENTS

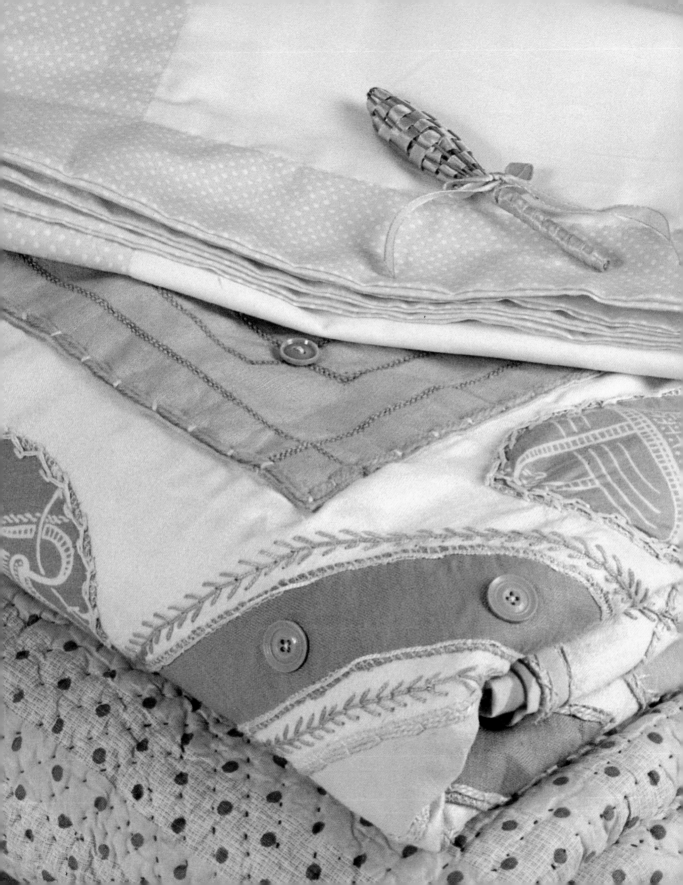

Introduction

FOR ME, THE SIGHT of a linen cupboard is a particularly satisfying one, the shelves piled high with freshly laundered bed linen, bundles of pillowcases stacked and tied like parcels with lengths of satin ribbon, clean table linen with napkins all folded, starched and ironed, ready for use. Even though the cupboard is merely a place to store things, the contents and their arrangement hold a special attraction. The practical and everyday items that are in constant use sit comfortably beside more distinguished pieces that are only allowed out on special occasions.

The traditional linen cupboard is one filled with fine linen and cotton in classic whites and creams with the occasional enticing glimpse of some exquisite hand-worked detail or embellishment like an openwork hem or an embroidered monogram, but that isn't the whole story. The heirloom look is not necessarily to everyone's taste and the whole function of the linen cupboard is that it isn't just for show, its beauty lies in its usefulness. New things can be added to the linen cupboard so that it becomes an ever-evolving collection of the contemporary and the retro, with a place for color and pattern.

Pure linen is a particularly durable material so there are still lots of old and antique examples to be found in a good, usable condition. Old linen, possesses a particularly appealing quality but is not always usable in its original form. Antique hemp and heavy textured linen sheets would not be my first choice to sleep between but the fabrics are too good to discard and can be reused in other ways; to make wonderful bedthrows, curtains and slip covers for chairs. Embroidered monograms can be incorporated into the chair back, on seat covers or used to make cushions.

Following this ethos, several of the projects in this book make use of secondhand cotton and linen remnants which were ridiculously cheap finds in second-hand shops. The projects follow traditional lines that are comfortable to live with but are intended to capture a contemporary feel. I hope you will find them worthy additions to your linen cupboard.

Gloria Nicol

The softly faded colors of old linen have a charm all of their own.

The History of Linen

CRISPLY LAUNDERED OR SOFTLY crumpled, linen is one of the most sophisticated natural textiles. A strong fabric with a wonderfully smooth finish, it is ideal for use in all types of soft furnishings, bed and table linens and clothing.

Linen is made from the long fibers of the flax plant *Linum usitatissimum*. The inner bark of this plant contains the long, slender fiber strands which are spun into a dirt-resistant and hard-wearing thread. Linen is more expensive than cotton, the most common natural fabric, because flax is not as widely cultivated and a lengthier and more difficult treatment is required to turn the raw fibers into finished cloth.

Traditionally, France, Holland and Belgium have been famous for growing fine quality flax, with different types of linen taking their name from the town or region in which they were woven, for example, cambric came from Cambrai, dowlas from Dourlas in Picardy and Holland linen from the Netherlands. Today the greatest producer of flax is Russia, closely followed by China and various Baltic states. Egypt, once so famous for its flax production, has now become one of the world's smallest producers.

Left: Neatly tied bundles of freshly laundered linen – a pleasing sight after the weekly wash is completed.

Right: Made from remnants of ticking, this bag is the perfect repository for knitting needles and embroidery hoops.

It is widely thought that flax was the first plant fiber to be used by man for weaving textiles, and archaeological excavations in Syria, Iraq and Iran have produced evidence of flax spinning dating back to at least 8000-6000 BC. Egyptian tomb paintings which date from 1900 BC also provide fascinating pictorial information on the ancient methods of flax spinning.

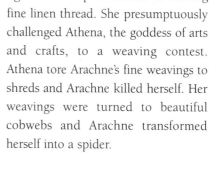

When Tutankhamen's tomb in Egypt's Valley of the Kings was first opened to the world by British archaeologists Lord Carnarvon and Howard Carter in 1922, it was found to contain linen curtains which had been placed there when the tomb was originally sealed in 1250 BC.

According to Egyptian mythology, it was believed that flax was created by the goddess Isis, sister-wife of the god Osiris. Isis used flax to weave sheets of linen to make a shroud for Osiris after his death at the hands of his brother Set. Accordingly, the priests who served her wore clean white linen as a symbol of purity. The tradition continues to this day, with the vestments worn by Catholic priests including a long white linen tunic. Greek mythology has its own legends surrounding Arachne, a young Greek girl with exceptional skills in weaving fine linen thread. She presumptuously challenged Athena, the goddess of arts and crafts, to a weaving contest. Athena tore Arachne's fine weavings to shreds and Arachne killed herself. Her weavings were turned to beautiful cobwebs and Arachne transformed herself into a spider.

Above: At one time monograms were stitched on all the household linen.

Left: An example of the fine detail that makes linen such a collectable item.

The ancient Egyptians used finely woven linen as shrouds and mummy wrappings, while a heavier weight of linen was pleated into kilts for men. Closely woven linen cloth was worn by the Phoenicians in battle as its toughness acted as armour, providing vital protection for soldiers.

As the Roman empire expanded, linen weaving spread into many parts of Europe, including Spain, Italy, Germany and Great Britain, and became part of European culture. From the early Middle Ages right up to the end of the eighteenth century, it was common for each country household to grow enough flax for its own needs. In fact, in eighth-century France under the reign of Charlemagne, or Charles I, each household was ordered to weave enough linen for its own use. For centuries the spinning and weaving of the thread was primarily a task for the women of the house.

One of the best examples of embroidered linen is the Bayeux Tapestry – the wall hanging made by Matilda, wife of William the Conqueror, between 1067 and 1070. Its name is rather misleading, as it is a linen cloth about 230 feet (70 m) in length and 20 in (50 cm)wide, heavily embroidered in blue, green, red and yellow wool, with more than 70 scenes capturing vivid moments from the battle of Hastings.

The royal household's ledgers show that in 1232 Henry III ordered 625 yards of linen for Christmas tablecloths. The price per yard was equivalent to one man's daily wages. In 1336, in over just twelve months, 1,200 yards of English linen, 300 yards of Parisian linen and 1,400 yards of linen from Rheims were purchased for Edward III's wardrobe.

Right: Textures of linen range from the finest thread to the coarsest weave.

11

Linen printed with wood blocks was often used as wall hangings and room decoration in wealthy households from the fourteenth century onwards. White linen damask cloths were popular in the sixteenth century. Still considered luxury items today, they are now mainly woven in Ireland, England and France. Whitework embroidery was used extensively throughout Europe from the sixteenth century.

In the seventeenth century linen weaving spread from the European mainland to Britain, as French and Flemish weavers escaping from religious persecution fled to Britain, bringing valuable skills and the latest equipment with them. The linen trade spread to England, Scotland and Ireland, and Ireland is still the home of Britain's linen industry today. As well as weaving fine linen for use in clothing, the mills produced many different qualities of cloth, including canvas for sail cloth and coarsely woven cloth for use as seed and grain bags.

In 1810 Napoleon I offered a reward of one million francs to the person who could invent a flax-spinning machine. Philippe de Girard devised such a machine and later established a spinning mill near Vienna.

In Britain, the second half of the eighteenth century saw the arrival of the Industrial Revolution. This led to a slow but steady decline in the demand

Left: An unusual two-colored mongram sits above an ornate border embroidered in cross stitch.

Right: These rich red mongrams are sewn in minute cross stitch and simple stem stitch.

for linen, as the newly mechanised mills could produce cotton cloth. The advantage of cotton was that it was cheaper to weave and far easier to launder. However, linen was still used for uniforms due to its strength and durability, and the American Civil War between 1861 and 1865 saw an increased demand for linen.

A long-standing tradition found around the world, and indeed one which still continues to this day in some countries, is the provision of a linen dowry for brides, also known in some countries as 'the bottom drawer'. This consisted of providing a chest full of the very best quality linen for the bride, from sheets and pillowcases to tablecloths and dish towels. Much of this linen would be hand-embroidered with the initials of the bride and groom, and sometimes the date of the wedding, and would be the most handsome items in the linen cupboard.

Care and Repair

To DISTINGUISH LINEN FROM COTTON, moisten a fingertip and touch the fabric. If it is linen, moisture will show on the other side almost immediately; if it is cotton, it will take longer for moisture to seep through.

It is inevitable that, at some point, wine will be spilled on your best white table linen. White wine can simply be washed out, but red wine stains need immediate action. This is one of those cases where the old tried-and-tested remedy is still the best. Treat the stain straight away by pouring a glass of white wine over it. This will neutralize the red wine. Next, rinse the cloth in warm water and then leave it to soak in a bowl of warm water to which borax had been added (use 1 tablespoon/15 ml of borax to 1 pint of water/600 ml). The fabric can then be machine-washed. If the stain has dried without being treated, soak it in the water and borax solution to loosen the stain before laundering.

An old remedy to whiten linen and remove stains – add a few slices of lemon to the wash tub when washing them. And more advice from the household manuals of yesterday – to remove ink stains from linen and calico, simply squeeze a few drops of lemon juice onto the stain. The ink will then disappear when the item is washed.

To remove candle wax or grease spots from table linen, first leave wax to harden and then carefully pick away as much as possible with a flat-bladed knife or with your fingernail. Next, cover the mark with a sheet of clean blotting paper and press with a hot iron until the wax melts. Repeat with another sheet of paper until the stain has vanished and then wash the cloth at the hottest temperature possible.

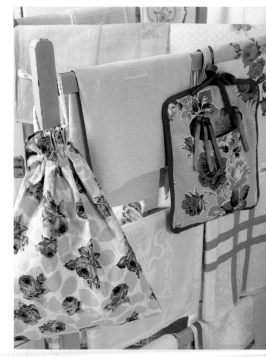

The weekly washday in an old-fashioned kitchen – neatly ironed dish towels and tablecloths air on a wooden clothes horse.

Overleaf: Hanging from a washing line strung between two apple trees, this freshly laundered linen dries in the early morning sun.

To restore a favorite piece of linen affected by mildew, the old remedy was to dampen the fabric and rub the spots with soap, then cover with fine chalk powder. The powder was rubbed in well and then the cloth was left to bleach outdoors in the sun. Today, a quicker method is to wash the stain out by treating the wrong side of the fabric with a solution of 4 teaspoons of bleach diluted in 1 pint (600 ml) of cool water.

Nowadays, with a sometimes confusing array of washing powders and liquids, it is far easier and quicker to clean linen items. With the exception of dark colors, linen can be machine-laundered on a hot wash and then pressed with a hot iron. Fragile pieces of linen should either be hand-washed or placed in a pillowcase before machine-washing.

In days gone by, large households employed armies of staff simply to keep the house running smoothly. With staff ranging in superiority from the housekeeper down to the humblest kitchen maid, there would sometimes be laundry maids whose sole task was to care for the household linens. Without the benefit of today's labor-saving machines, the laundry was a full-time occupation. The process started with making the detergents using recipes such as this one.

Place half a pound of soda in an earthenware pan and pour on two quarts of boiling water. Finely shred half a pound of household soap and place in a second saucepan with two quarts of cold water. Place this over a gentle heat until it boils. When the soap has completely dissolved, pour the liquid into the pan containing the soda mixture. Mix well and leave to cool. When set, it will form a strong soap jelly which can be added to the washing water.

For the best finish, press items while they are still very damp. The pressed surface can become rather shiny, so whenever possible iron items on the wrong side. If cotton or linen items become scorched, try rubbing the marks with lemon juice and then leaving them in sunlight to fade naturally. Scorch marks on the plate of the iron can be removed by rubbing it with a bar of soap while the iron is still warm. Polish off the soap with a clean cloth and the marks should disappear completely.

Starching linen not only gives it a crisper, smarter appearance, but also helps to protect it from stains as the coating on the fabric prevents them from being absorbed so easily. There are now many spray starches available

When darning linen, always use cotton rather than acrylic thread, and use pre-shrunk fabrics when patching cloths.

Darning

1 Choose a thread that matches the fabric being repaired and on the right side of the fabric, make a row of running stitches below the hole to be darned. Take the thread backwards and forwards across the hole in closely spaced rows, ensuring that the fabric stays flat. Anchor each row with a small stitch at the side of the hole.

2 Weave the thread up and down through the horizontal threads, going over one thread and under the next. At the end of each row, anchor the thread with a small stitch at the side of the hole.

Patching

1 Trim the edges of the hole to make a neat square or rectangle and clip the corners to a depth of ¼ in (5 mm). Cut a patch to fit over the hole allowing an extra ½ in (1 cm) all around. Turn under a ¼ in (5 mm) hem and press. Stitch the patch over the hole using running stitch in a thread that matches the fabric.

2 Turn the item over and on this side turn under the edges of the fabric by ¼ in (5 mm) and press. Overstitch the turned edges with tiny stitches.

in stores, but you could try making your own sugar starch. Add 4 tablespoons of white granulated sugar to a teacup of cold water. Allow the sugar to dissolve, then pour the solution into a bowl. Dip the dry linen article into the solution, reshape it, then leave to dry naturally. Linen starched in this way should not be ironed.

When linen has been washed, pressed and aired, store it away interspersed with small bags made of silk, muslin or cotton filled with an aromatic mixture of herbs such as lavender, thyme or southernwood, plus rose petals for a floral scent or cedar shavings or crushed cloves for spicier overtones. These will help to keep moths and other insects at bay. Replace the dried herbs in the bags when their scent begins to fade.

Linen should ideally be stored in a dark, dry, cool cupboard (the airing cupboard is probably too warm). The fabric needs to be able to breathe so do not wrap it in polyethylene to keep it dust-free. Instead, wrap it in white, acid-free tissue paper. Small items can simply be stored on a flat shelf, interleaved with sheets of tissue paper. Larger items, such as table-cloths, should be rolled around a large cardboard tube after pressing (the tubes from inside rolls of fabric are ideal) to prevent creases. The tube should be wrapped in a layer of white, acid-free tissue paper first. Roll a layer of tissue paper between the layers of the fabric. Place the tube on a flat surface out of daylight.

Old linen which is showing signs of wear and tear can be repaired in a number of ways. Items which have simply worn thin can be carefully patched with matching fabric on the

The texture and structure of linen cloths are some of its most attractive features, giving it a strength and flexibility of use.

underside, or can be carefully darned in the old-fashioned way. To give new life and a new look to linen items such as bedcovers, tablecloths or napkins, try patching with small squares of contrasting fabric. Attach them to the main cloth with simply embroidery stitches.

If you buy or inherit any pieces of old linen which you think may be valuable or may need special care, consult an expert before attempting to repair or clean them yourself. Museums or auction houses should be able to put you in touch with the relevant conservation or valuation experts.

Cheerful linens complement bright china and provide decorative touches in a hard-working kitchen, from the star-patterned shelf edging to the checked curtain which hides the buckets and washing powders stored below the sink.

Making
the most
of Linen

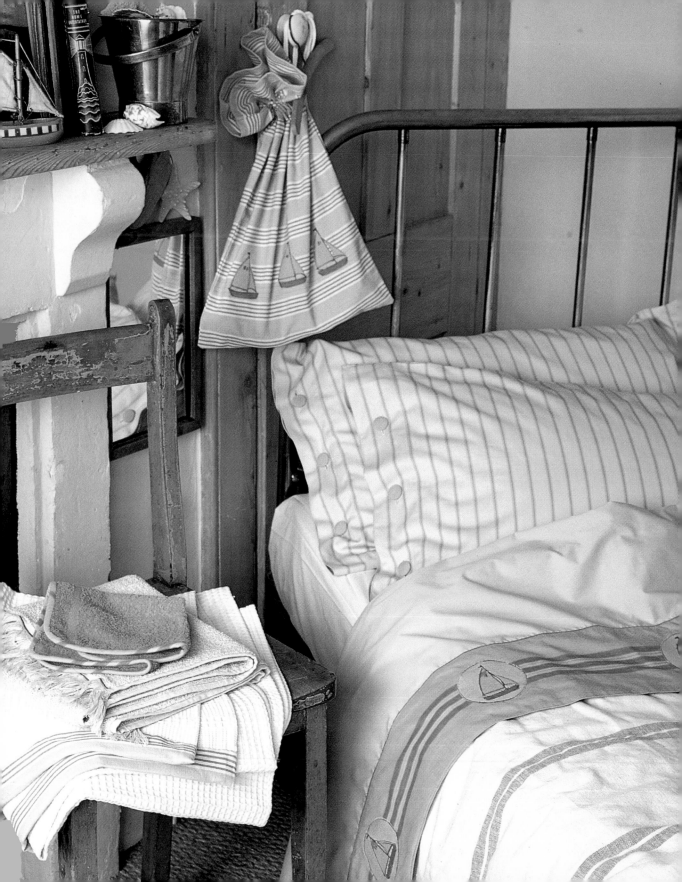

Children's Bed Linen

Give your children's bed linen a personal touch by adding an appliqué decoration. Choose motifs to reflect their interests or hobbies – here sailing boats have been used, but you could easily substitute airplanes, animals, trains, teddies, favorite toys or their initials.

The striped ticking fabric used for the pillowcases and the bedcover give a traditional look to the room, a theme which has been carried through to the towels with a fabric border and the flannel edged with a bias stripe. The boat appliqué has been applied to the top edge of the sheet, but could also be added to the pillowcases, a dressing gown pocket or the bedcover for a fully coordinated look. You could use this idea in a living room or dining room, by adding motifs to cushion covers, curtain tiebacks or a tablecloth.

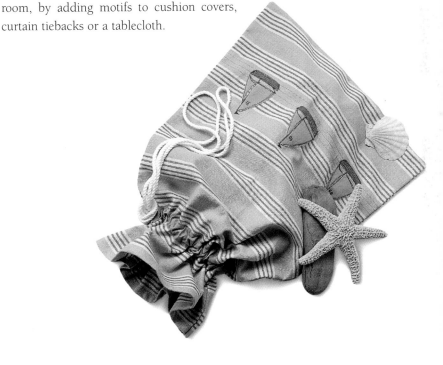

A simple drawstring bag with an appliquéd decoration makes the perfect home for pajamas, play shoes, toys or a treasured collection of seashells.

Boat-edged Sheet

The boat-appliquéd turnback is applied to a standard single sheet. Calculate fabric quantities to fit other sizes of sheet.

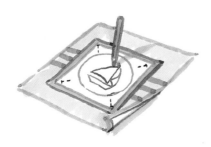

YOU WILL NEED:

a single sheet

71 in (180 cm) striped cotton fabric measuring 48 in (122 cm) wide

20 in (50 cm) square of plain cotton fabric

20 in (50 cm) square of fusible bonding web

contrasting and matching threads

pins

embroidery hoop

dressmakers' carbon paper

embroidery scissors

sewing machine

1 For the turnback, cut a strip of striped fabric to fit along the top of the sheet. It should measure the width of the sheet by 12 in (30 cm) deep, plus a further ⅝ in (1.5 cm) seam allowance on all sides. The strip will be folded in half lengthways, so consider how the stripes will run before cutting the fabric. Trace the boat design from the template on page 77 onto pattern paper. Press a piece of fusible bonding web to the back of a scrap of the striped fabric. Using dressmakers' carbon paper, transfer the shapes from the boat design on to the backed fabric and cut out five sets of the boat sails and hull.

2 Cut the plain fabric into five square pieces which fit the embroidery hoop with a bit of extra fabric all around. Remove the paper backing from the fusible bonding web and pin then iron a pair of sails and a hull to the fabric. Select the free embroidery mode on the sewing machine and attach a darning foot. Place the fabric in the hoop and appliqué the boat sections into position, using rows of darning stitches freestyle to embroider and fill the hull and outline the sails, adding a flag at the top, a number on the main sail and some rigging as required. Remove the appliqué from the hoop. Work each of the five motifs in the same way.

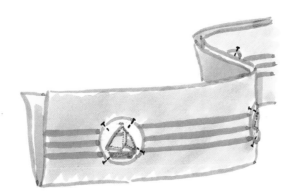

3 Press fusible bonding web to the back of each appliquéd square. From the template, trace the circles around the boats and cut each boat circle out. Wrong sides facing, fold the striped strip in half lengthways and press the fold. Making one side of the folded strip the right side of the turnback, press under the seam allowance. Pin one appliquéd circle in the center and two other circles, evenly spaced, on either side, with the boat hulls nearest the fold. Remove the paper backing and iron the circles in place. Set the sewing machine to zig zag and work a narrow satin stitch around the edge of each circle.

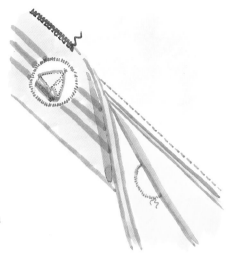

The towels shown on page 26 have been edged with contrasting fabric bias strips or highlighted with a simple line of machine-worked satin stitch to coordinate with the bed linen set.

4 Press under the seam allowance along the underside edge of the turnback. Right sides facing, fold the turnback in half lengthways, matching side edges, and stitch down each side, catching in the pressed seam allowances. Trim the seams, clip the corners and turn right side out. Cut any hem away from the top edge of the sheet. With the underside of the turnback facing the wrong side of the sheet, pin then stitch the turnback in place. Trim the seam and press it towards the turnback. Fold the turnback over to the right side and pin in place. With the machine set for zig zag, work a narrow satin stitch line along the edge of the border to secure. Top stitch close to the side and folded edges to finish.

Boat Shoebag

YOU WILL NEED:

28 in (70 cm) fabric measuring 45 in (115 cm) wide

a thin strip of contrasting fabric

scraps of plain fabric for the appliqué

fusible bonding web

dressmakers' carbon paper

contrasting and matching threads

pins

embroidery scissors

sewing machine

86 in (220 cm) cord

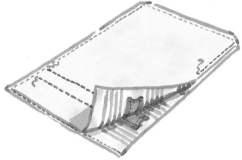

1 Cut two rectangles of fabric 21 x 14 in (53 x 36 cm) for the front and back of the bag. Trace the boat design from the template on page 77 onto pattern paper. Press fusible bonding web to the back of a scrap of plain fabric and a scrap of contrasting fabric. Using dressmakers' carbon paper, transfer the design to the backed fabrics and cut three sets of boat sails from plain fabric and three hulls from contrasting fabric. Stitch three evenly spaced lines, in a contrasting color, across the bag front approximately 4¼ in (11 cm) up from the bottom edge. Appliqué the boats to the bag front in the same way as those for the turnback.

2 Cut two strips 13½ x 1½ in (34 x 4 cm) from the contrasting fabric for the cord pocket. Turn under and stitch ¼ in (5 mm) along the short edges. Turn under ¼ in (5 mm) along both long edges and press. Place one strip across the bag front 4¼ in (11 cm) down from the top edge and ⅝ in (1.5 cm) in from each side edge, then top stitch close to the top and bottom edges. Stitch the cord pocket to the bag back in the same position.

3 Stitch a hem of ¼ in (5 mm) then ½ in (1 cm) along the top edges of the front and back of the bag. Right sides facing, pin then stitch down both sides and along the bottom edge, taking a seam of ⅝ in (1.5 cm). Press open and neaten seams. Cut the cord into two equal lengths and thread one cord through each cord pocket. Tie the ends together into flat knots then pull the knots inside the pockets.

Ticking Pillowcases with Covered Buttons

To fit standard pillow,
30 x 20 in (75 x 50 cm)

1 Cut out two rectangles of ticking 36 x 21¼ in (91 x 53 cm). Right sides facing, pin then stitch the rectangles together along both long edges and one short edge, taking seam allowances of ⅝ in (1.5 cm). Press the seams open, trim the corners and turn to the right side. Turn under and press the seam allowance along the open edge then trim the pressed seam allowance to ½ in (1 cm).

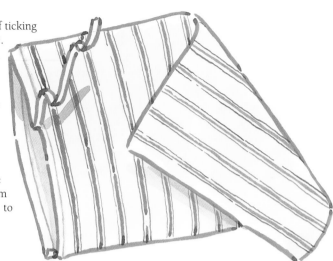

YOU WILL NEED:

43 in (110 cm) ticking measuring 45 in (115 cm) wide for each pillowcase

3 cover buttons

a scrap of plain fabric

needle and thread

pins

sewing machine

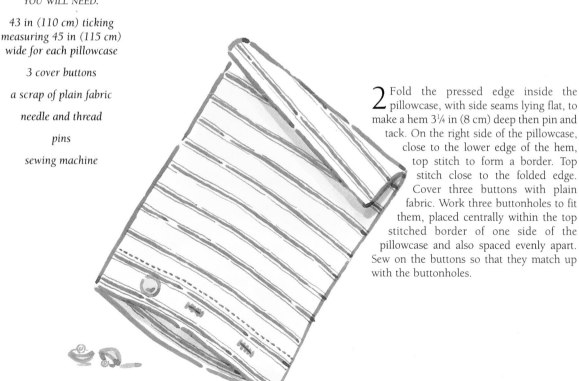

2 Fold the pressed edge inside the pillowcase, with side seams lying flat, to make a hem 3¼ in (8 cm) deep then pin and tack. On the right side of the pillowcase, close to the lower edge of the hem, top stitch to form a border. Top stitch close to the folded edge. Cover three buttons with plain fabric. Work three buttonholes to fit them, placed centrally within the top stitched border of one side of the pillowcase and also spaced evenly apart. Sew on the buttons so that they match up with the buttonholes.

Tea Cozy

SIMPLE EMBROIDERY IN STEM STITCH and satin stitch adorns this reassuringly plump tea cozy with its edging of cheerful pom-poms. The cosy is made in three layers – lining, batting and a medium-weight linen for the outer layer – and the linen can be removed for laundering. The pom-poms can be bought attached to a length of braid so that they do not have to be sewn on individually.

The linen is cut to size and embroidered before the tea cozy is stitched together. A thick perlé thread is used so the embroidery grows quickly. Roses in the style of Charles Rennie Mackintosh are embroidered in blocks of satin stitch, while the stems and leaves are sewn in stem stitch.

If coffee is your favored beverage, pattern pieces can be drawn to fit a tall, slimmer coffeepot rather than a stouter teapot. If you wish, you could make miniature cosies to sit atop boiled eggs for the breakfast table.

Sophisticated shades of beige and pale green have been used to create this stylish tea cozy – perfect for tea in the garden.

Tea Cozy

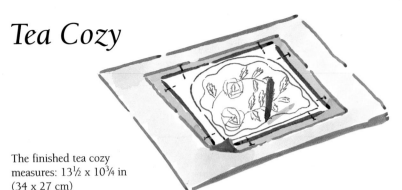

The finished tea cozy measures: 13½ x 10¾ in (34 x 27 cm)

YOU WILL NEED:

16 in (40 cm) of medium-weight linen measuring 36 in (90 cm) wide

32 in (80 cm) cotton lining fabric measuring 36 in (90 cm) wide

16 in (40 cm) batting measuring 36 in (90 cm) wide

36 in (90 cm) bobble fringing

perlé No 3 & No 5 embroidery thread in matching colors

sewing and embroidery needles

tracing paper

dressmakers' carbon paper

sewing thread

pins

sewing machine

1 Copy the design onto tracing paper from the template on page 77. Cut out front and back pieces in linen, allowing 2 in (5 cm) extra fabric all around the edges. Using dressmakers' carbon paper in a color close to the fabric, pin the pattern to the front piece and slip the carbon between them, carbon side to the right side of the linen. Carefully trace the design onto the linen. Transfer the design to the back piece in the same way.

2 Embroider the front and back pieces, working the roses in blocks of satin stitch using perlé No 3 and the border, stems and leaves in stem stitch using perlé No 5. Trim the linen to give ⅝ in (1.5 cm) seam allowance all round. To make the linen top, with right sides facing, pin the front and back together around the curved edge and stitch. Turn right side out and press, taking care not to flatten the embroidery. Turn the seam allowance to the inside on the bottom edge and tack.

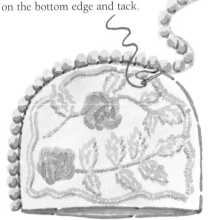

3 To make the tea cozy lining, cut out four pieces of lining fabric following the pattern with an extra ⅝ in (1.5 cm) allowed on all edges for seams, and two pieces of batting, cut without seam allowances. For the inside lining, pin the batting to the wrong side of two of the lining pieces within the seam allowance and fix in place with loose slip stiches along the batting edges. Right sides facing, pin these two lining pieces together and stitch around the curved edge. Trim the seam to ½ in (1 cm) and turn the bottom edge seam allowance to the wrong side and press.

4 For the outside lining, right sides facing, pin two lining pieces together and stitch around the curved edge. Trim the seam, turn right side out and press. Turn under the seam allowance along the bottom edge and press. Push the inside lining into the outside lining slip stitch together along the bottom edge. Slip stitch the bobble fringing to the linen top, along the curved edge, then push the lining inside the tea cozy top, matching bottom edges. Slip stitch the top to the lining along the bottom edge.

Old damask linen napkins in softly faded pastel hues, neatly pressed and tied with contrasting ribbons, ready to provide the perfect finishing touch for the table.

Monogrammed Pajamas

ONOGRAMS ARE THE PERFECT way to personalize an item of clothing or bed or table linen – a single initial of a Christian name, the family surname or the entwined initials of a bride and groom. Add monograms to pillowcases, sheets, hand towels, face flannels, handkerchiefs, napkins – the list is endless. White thread stitched onto a white background looks particularly effective. You can either use the alphabet of letters given on pages 41-43 (this has been used on the pair of pajamas shown here) or look through books and magazines for letters in different styles. The napkins shown on pages 42-43 are sewn in cross stitch. Waste canvas is tacked onto the napkin – this gives you a grid to work to and helps you count the threads. When the monogram has been stitched, pull the waste canvas away thread by thread.

A pajama pocket neatly embroidered with a monogram turns an everyday item of clothing into something special.

Mono-grammed Pajamas

An embroidered monogram can be worked on the pocket of an existing pair of pajamas but the pocket will need to be removed first. Stitch spare fabric around the edges of the pocket so that it is big enough to be held firmly in an embroidery hoop and remove the fabric after the embroidery is completed. Alternatively, as we did here, follow a dressmakers' pattern and make the pajamas from scratch. Work the monogram onto a piece of fabric bigger than the pocket pattern piece and cut it out to size when the embroidery is complete.

1 Mark out the dimensions of the pocket pattern piece centrally on the fabric. Trace the letters required from the alphabet shown on pages 41-43, placing the letters together in a staggered arrangement, slightly overlapping with the loops intertwined.

2 Pin the traced letters onto the fabric, placing them centrally within the pocket outline. Place the carbon paper between the tracing paper and fabric, carbon side down then trace the letters onto the fabric, pressing down hard with a sharp pencil.

YOU WILL NEED:

10 in (25 cm) square piece of fabric

tracing paper

dressmakers' carbon paper

embroidery hoop

stranded cotton embroidery thread

needle and thread

pins

pencil

embroidery scissors

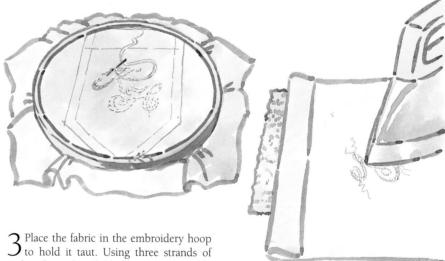

3 Place the fabric in the embroidery hoop to hold it taut. Using three strands of embroidery thread throughout, work in backstitch along the outlines of the letters. Then embroider each letter in satin stitch, working over the backstitched, outlines to give raised edges.

4 Remove the hoop and press the fabric lightly on the back, placing the embroidery face down on a towel to prevent the stitches becoming flattened. Make up the pocket using the pattern instructions and stitch in place on the pajamas.

*These monogrammed initials make it easy to identify these
pajamas at a glance.*

S
T
U
V
W
X
Y
Z

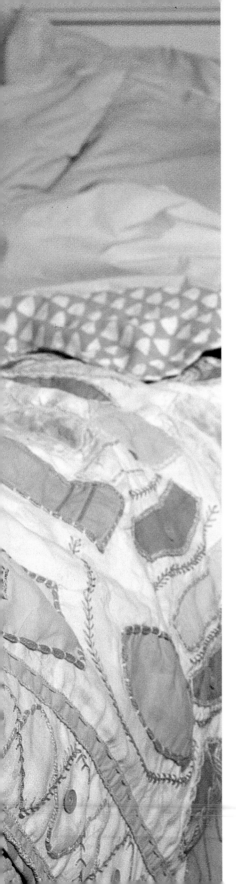

Appliquéd Quilt

A̲T FIRST GLANCE, this colorful bed cover looks likes a version of crazy patchwork, but look closer and you will see that it is, in fact, a form of appliqué, which is much faster to do. A large cream damask tablecloth has been given a new life by backing it with a length of cotton lining and a layer of quilt batting.

The appliquéd shapes have been cut from scraps of fabric found in the remnant bag, from old table mats and napkins and from favorite clothes which have worn out. The pieces are randomly machine-stitched into place with a zig zag stitch (this means they do not need to be hemmed first) and then embellished with embroidery stitches. Spaces between the shapes have been filled with more embroidery, creating a busy, jewel-like effect.

A treasured collection of old buttons, built up over the years, provides the final finishing touches. The buttons have been sewn through all three layers of the quilt to hold them together.

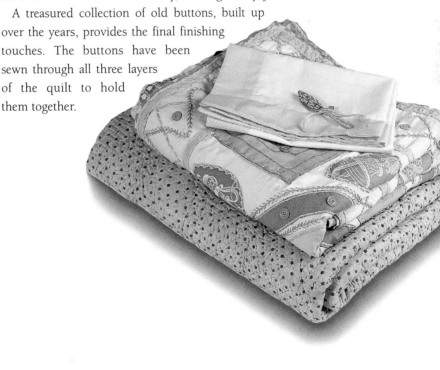

A quilt to treasure, made with scraps of fabrics that hold precious memories.

Appliquéd Quilt

There are several methods suitable for joining the fabric pieces onto the background fabric so choose the one that suits you. For quick results, cut the fabric pieces to size, pin them in position and stitch them with a close zig zag stitch on the sewing machine. Alternatively, cut the shapes adding an extra ½ in (1 cm) all round for turnings. Turn under and press the allowances to the wrong side, clipping the curves where necessary, then pin in place on the background fabric and hand or machine stitch in place.

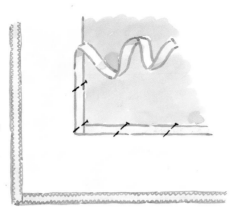

1 Cut long continous strips of fabric, approximately ¾ in (2 cm) wide. Lay the background fabric down flat and place the strips all around the outer edges, joining strips where necessary, then pin and stitch in place. Cut more strips of fabric and join to the background in the same way, approximately 4¼ in (11 cm) inside the outer line, to make a border.

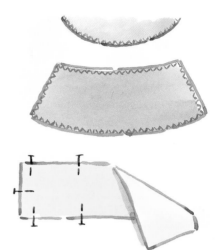

2 Cut the scraps of fabric into different shapes and place them on the background in a simple design, radiating out from a central circle with a loose symmetry out towards the sides and corners. Make the most of any embroidery, monograms or interesting patterns in the fabric scraps when cutting them out and use them in the design. Pin then stitch the shapes in position.

YOU WILL NEED:

background fabric, we used a damask tablecloth 45 x 70 in (115 x 175 cm)

an assortment of fabric scraps

stranded cotton and perlé No 5 embroidery threads

needles and thread

pins

medium-weight cotton backing fabric the same size as the background fabric plus 4 in (10 cm) on each side

cotton quilt batting the same size as background fabric

buttons

thimble

safety pins

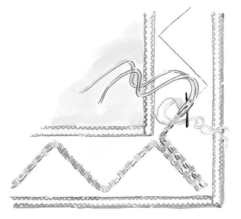

3 Draw a continuous zig zag line very lightly in pencil within the border lines and couch threads in place over the line. Embroider another zig zag line in fly stitch to work over and between the couched lines to make a series of diamond shapes within the border. Work rows of continuous cross stitches along the outer edge of the border and long running stitches along the other border edges.

4 Embellish the appliqué shapes with embroidery as required, using couched thread lines, fly stitch and feather stitches following the edges of the shapes and fly stitch and double feather stitch bands and borders worked onto the background fabric surrounding the shapes. Press the quilt top.

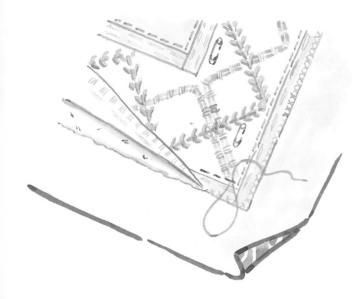

5 Lay the backing fabric down flat, wrong side up. Lay the cotton batting flat on top of that just within the fabrics edges, then lay the appliquéd top right side up on top, matching the edges with the backing. Flatten the layers out and join them together with safety pins fastened through all layers at regular intervals. Join the layers together by working rows of small running stitches that go right through all the layers to the backing fabric, following the inside and outside edges of the border and around the edges of some of the shapes at regular intervals.

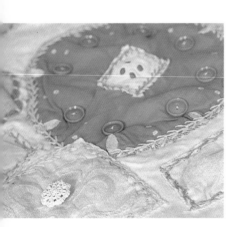

6 Cut the backing fabric to 1 in (2.5 cm) bigger than the quilt top and turn it inside the quilt, pin then slip stitch the top to the backing to secure. Stitch a button into the center of alternate diamond shapes within the border all around, stitching through all layers. Place buttons on some of the fabric shapes to become part of the overall design, sometimes a single button within a shape or several around the edges of a circle, and stitch them in place to hold the layers together. Remove the safety pins.

STITCHES – *see page 76.*
Couching
Blanket stitch
Feather and double feather stitches
Fly stitch
Running stitch

Lavender Bottle

THESE OLD-FASHIONED lavender bottles, with their flowerheads carefully enclosed within the lavender stems, are far simpler to make than you might at first realize. Make them with fresh lavender (the stems need to be flexible as they must be bent over) and then leave them to dry naturally.

Lavender bottles can be used to decorate a linen cupboard or a lingerie drawer or to add a scent to bundles of clean linen. The flowers will retain their fragrance for a long time – simply squeeze the bottle gently to release more scent. As well as looking decorative, the powerful, aromatic odor of these bottles will keep moths and other insects away from the linen cupboard.

Each lavender bottle requires a large amount of ribbon. You can use wide or narrow ribbon, though if you use narrow ribbon you will need a greater amount. If you wish, the stems can be left unbound.

Sitting atop a pile of freshly laundered linen, this lavender bottle will add a heavenly scent as well as keeping moths at bay.

Lavender Bottle

YOU WILL NEED:

30 stems of fresh lavender, at least 12 in (30 cm) in length

sewing thread

elastic band

80 in (200 cm) of ¼ in (5 mm) wide narrow ribbon

needle

narrow bodkin

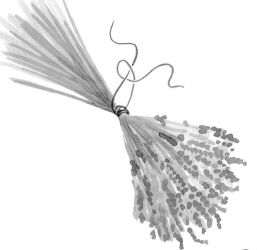

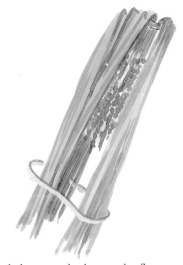

1 Hold the stems together so that the flower heads are all bunched together and wrap sewing thread tightly around the stems just below the flowers, tying the ends with a knot.

2 Bend the stems back over the flowers from where the thread holds them, so that the flowers become encased by the stems and place an elastic band around the stems to keep them together.

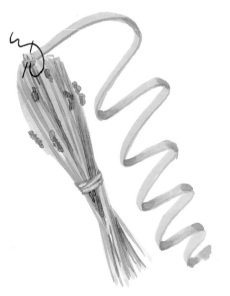

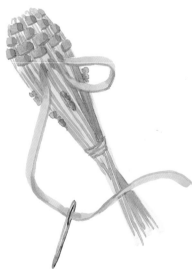

3 Take a length of narrow ribbon and wrap one end around a stem at the top of the bottle, fixing it in place with a few stitches with a needle and thread.

4 Treating a pair of stems as one, weave the ribbon in and out between each pair of stems all around the bulb of the bottle, using a bodkin to pull the ribbon through. Fasten off the end of the ribbon with a few stitches. Wrap ribbon twice around the stems, near the ends, knot it then cut the ends short. Remove the elastic band and tie a short length of contrastingly colored, wider ribbon twice around the stems and in a bow.

Wave-edged Tablecloth and Napkins

THREE DIFFERENT BUT COMPLEMENTARY fabrics have been used here to create this attractive wave-edged cloth and matching napkins. A floral-printed material with a cream background makes up the central area of the cloth, with a plain terracotta shade used for the deep border, edged with bias binding. The border has been cut with a gently scalloped edge to add extra detail and to allow the cloth to drape softly. Linen is an ideal fabric for table linen as it can withstand frequent laundering.

The napkins have a contrasting bias edging and can be made from offcuts of matching or contrasting fabrics. Although made for a small, round table, the idea could be adapted to fit a larger square or rectangular dining table.

Nestling in the shade of an apple tree, this linen-covered table provides the perfect spot for a summer lunch.

Tablecloth

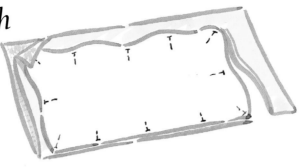

The finished tablecloth measures approximately 60 in (150 cm) square.

YOU WILL NEED:

48 in (120 cm) main fabric measuring 56 in (140 cm) wide

60 in (150 cm) contrasting border fabric measuring 56 in (140 cm) wide

40 in (100 cm) fabric for bias edging measuring 56 in (140 cm) wide

pattern paper

needle and thread

sewing machine

ruler

1 Draw the pattern pieces to size from the template on page 77. For the main part of the tablecloth fold a large sheet of paper in half then draw out the shape with one of the straight edges against the fold to make a pattern for half of the cloth. Fold the fabric in half and pin the straight edge of the pattern to the fold then cut out. For the border, fold a long strip of paper in half widthways then draw out the border pattern with the straight edge against the fold to make one border section. Cut out four border pieces from the contrasting fabric.

2 To make the bias edging, fold the edging fabric in half lengthways, pin together side edges then stitch to make a tube. Press the seam open and lay the tube down flat. Draw a straight line running across the fabric at 45° from the top open end of the tube to the bottom. Draw more lines parallel to the first one 2½ in (6 cm) apart. Cut down the tube along one of the lines to open it up, then cut along all the other lines to make bias strips. Join the strips together to make a long, and continuous bias ribbon.

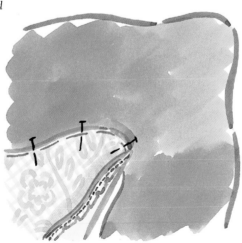

3 Stay stitch all round the edge of the main part of the tablecloth ½ in (1 cm) in from the edge. Clip all along the edge at regular intervals up to the stitching then turn under ⅝ in (1.5 cm) all around the cloth, tack and press. With right sides facing, join the four border sections together to form a frame with mitered corners. Lay the border down flat, right side up, then place the main part of the tablecloth in the center so that the edges are overlap the inside edges of the border by ⅝ in (1.5 cm). Pin in place and tack, then top stitch close to the edge.

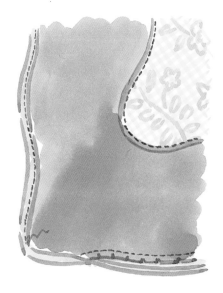

4 Press under ⅝ in (1.5 cm) along one edge of the bias edging and trim the turning to ¼ in (5 mm). With right sides of edging to the wrong side of the border, pin the unturned edge of the bias edging along the wavy edge of the border and stitch together all the way round until the edging meets. Trim and turn under the end to overlap where they meet. Trim the seam to ¼ in (5 mm) and clip at regular intervals. Press the seam flat towards the binding then fold the edging over the seam so that the folded edge meets the stitched seam line and pin in place. Top stitch all around the binding close to the fold to complete the cloth and press flat.

Napkins

Each finished napkin measures approximately 17½ in (44 cm) square.

YOU WILL NEED:

20 in (50 cm) fabric measuring 56 in (140 cm) wide

20 in (50 cm) fabric for bias edging measuring 54 in (140 cm) wide

pattern paper

needle and thread

sewing machine

ruler

1 Draw the pattern piece to size from the template on page 77. The template shows a quarter of the napkin so fold the pattern paper in half and draw out the napkin shape with a straight edge against the fold to make a pattern of half the napkin. Fold the fabric in half and pin the pattern with the straight edge against the fold to cut out the whole napkin shape.

2 Make the bias edging as explained in step 2 of the tablecloth. Press under a ⅝ in (1.5 cm) long one edge of the bias edging and trim the turning to ¼ in (5 mm). With the right side of edging facing the wrong side of the napkin, pin the unturned edge of the bias edging along the edge of the napkin and stitch together all the way round. Trim and turn under the end to overlap where the ends meet. Trim the seam to ¼ in (5 mm) and clip at regular intervals. Press the seam flat towards the binding then fold the edging over the seam so that the pressed edge meets the stitched seam line and pin in place. Top stitch all around the edging close to the inside edge to complete the napkin.

Pastel Oxford Pillowcases

CRISP WHITE LINEN pillowcases with contrasting pastel-colored Oxford edges and smart button fastenings add a modern touch to a charming old-fashioned bedroom.

These pillowcases are fairly quick to make – the pattern pieces are all simple shapes, all the sewing is in straight lines and once you have mastered the art of making one, you will be able to run up matching or contrasting pairs at speed. You could even use colored linen for the main body of the case, picking out colors to echo and complement the decoration of the bedroom, or a subtly patterned fabric. These pillowcases are also an ideal way to use up odd remnants of linen, or to pull together various colors used in the room's decor. You could also use strips of the colored fabric to add matching borders to the top edge of sheets.

Here cream fabric buttons have been used to close the pillowcases, but if you have a button-covering kit, try making buttons to match the color of the borders.

Piles of soft pillows, covered with soft pastel-colored linen pillowcases, turn a wrought-iron bedstead into a welcoming retreat.

Pastel Oxford Pillowcases

To fit standard pillow,
30 x 20 in (75 x 50 cm)

YOU WILL NEED:

*44 in (110 cm) white
chambray or fine linen,
measuring 54 in
(135 cm) wide*

*32 in (80 cm) chambray or
fine linen, measuring
44 in (112 cm) wide, in a
pastel color*

five buttons

needle and thread

pins

sewing machine

1 In white, cut a back 21¼ x 31 (53 x 78 cm) in, a front 21¼ x 28 in (53 x 71 cm) and a button flap 21¼ x 6 in (53 x 15 cm). In pastel fabric, cut a buttonhole band 21¼ x 3¼ in (53 x 8 cm). With the wrong side of the front facing right side of the band, stitch the band to the front. Press to right side. Turn under ½ in (1 cm) on the long edge and stitch to the front. Make five buttonholes.

2 Press under then sew a ½ in (1 cm), then 1 in (2 cm) hem along one long edge of the button flap. Wrong sides facing, place the flap on the pillowcase back. Place the pillowcase front also on the back so that the buttonhole edge overlaps the hemmed edge on the flap. Stitch all round the outside.

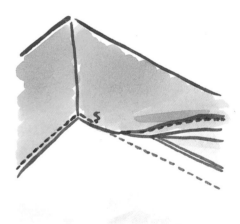

3 In pastel fabric cut two long and two short border pieces, following the directions in step 2 on page 70. The back seam line should be 5½ in (14 cm) from the front seam and the point should be 2¾ in (7 cm) beyond the ends of the seam lines. Stay stitch border pieces by sewing ⅝ in (1.5 cm) from front edges, then join them at the mitered corners.

4 Turn under and press a ⅝ in (1.5 cm) hem along the stay-stitched front edges. Right sides facing, sew the back edge of the border to the back of the pillowcase, pivoting the work at the corners. Press the seam towards the border. Fold the front edge of the border to the right side of the pillowcase and top stitch it in place to cover the sewing line. Sew on the buttons.

Linen Bags

STARCHED AND PRESSED to perfection, these neat bags sewn from finest linen or translucent cotton voile are ideal for use in the bedroom. Make them in a range of sizes and use them to hold camisoles and lingerie, silk stockings, lace-edged lawn handkerchiefs, pale kid gloves and the finest cotton nightdresses. These envelope-style bags have been made from remnants of subtly striped and checked fabric, edged with narrow binding and fastened with lengths of toning ribbon.

The fabric has been spray starched twice – once before cutting out the pieces and then again before pressing the finished item. This strengthens it, makes it easier to sew and gives it an extremely smart finish.

When made in an opaque fabric, these bags can also be used as a form of gift wrap with a present, such as scented sachets, a new lipstick or even a slim volume of poetry, neatly enclosed inside.

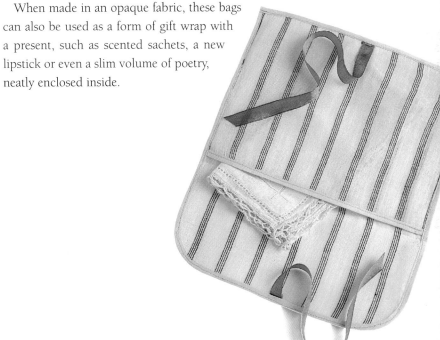

A collection of beautifully finished and pressed bags, each tied with a length of luxurious silk ribbon and each holding a piece of fine lingerie or lace, make a decorative and useful addition to the linen cupboard.

Linen Bags

The bags are made in three different sizes with finished measurements as follows:
A small bag 10 x 7 in (25 x 18 cm),
B large bag 17½ x 11 in (44 x 28 cm),
C long bag 10 x 13½ in (25 x 34 cm).
Cut out rectangles of linen or voile for the different bag sizes as follows:
A 18 ½ x 10 in (47 x 25 cm);
B 29½ x 17½ in (74 x 44 cm);
C 33 x 10 in (83 x 25 cm).

YOU WILL NEED:

*20 in (50 cm) of cotton voile or organdie measuring 43 in (107 cm) wide for bag **A**; 32 in (80 cm) for bag **B**; and 36 in (90 cm) for bag **C***

*60 in (150 cm) bias binding for **A**, 96 in (240 cm) for bags **B** & **C***

28 in (70 cm) ribbon measuring ½ in (1 cm) wide

spray starch

needle and thread

pins

sewing machine

1 Stiffen the fabric with spray starch and an iron. Lay the fabric flat then make a bottom fold across the width of the fabric, for **A** 7 in (18 cm); for **B** 11 in (28 cm); for **C** 13½ in (34 cm) up from a short edge. Fold the other short edge over this to form the flap and press to mark the folds. Cut the corners of the flap into matching curves.

2 Cut a strip of bias binding to fit across the inside straight edge, right across the width of the bag. Fold the binding in half lengthways, right side out, and press the fold. Push the binding over the straight edge so that the raw edge of the voile is completely enclosed, tack then top stitch in place close to the inside edge.

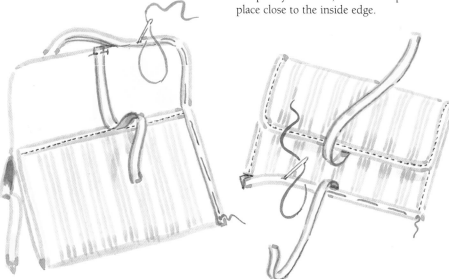

3 Refold the bottom fold with wrong sides facing and the flap open and tack the sides together. Cut the ribbon in half and pin one of the pieces to the wrong side of the middle of the flap, with raw edges matching and the ribbon lying in towards the inside of the bag. Bind the sides and along the edge of the flap with bias binding as before, turning under the raw short ends.

4 Pin the other piece of ribbon to the middle of the bottom folded edge, with the ribbon's raw edge to the fold and the ribbon running in towards the bag and tack in place. Bind along the bottom folded edge with bias binding as before. Trim the ribbon ends. Fold the flap over the bag and spray starch and iron again to give a crisp finish.

Wooden coathangers, covered with a layer of batting and gently gathered cotton chintz, bring a charmingly old-fashioned look to the most modern of wardrobes.

Velvet-edged Blanket

WITH THE POPULARITY of lightweight quilts and duvets, blankets have become sadly neglected, often to be found bundled at the back of the linen cupboard. However, woollen blankets are very expensive to buy and, with the right care, do last a long time, so give them a new lease of life by dyeing them an attractive color and adding a deep border of rich shot velvet. Embellish them with lengths of decorative ribbon or braid and add matching velvet roses to the corners, and the result is a glorious addition to your bedlinen which will do double duty as a sofa or chair throw.

To give them a modern, up-to-date look, these blankets have been dyed with cold water dyes (see the advice overleaf on choosing colors). Full-size blankets are usually too heavy to be dyed in a washing machine, so use a large plastic tub (often sold for use in the garden) or a new plastic garbage can. If any areas of the blanket have become moth-eaten, trim the blanket to a smaller size before dyeing.

Modern colors of soft aqua and lilac have given new life to these old blankets. The velvet trim adds a touch of luxury, transforming them from an everyday item to something to be coveted and cherished.

Velvet-edged Blanket

Old blankets can be dyed to produce rich, deep colors. When deciding what color to dye a blanket, consider its original color first and choose a deeper shade of a color in the same range to prevent muddy indistinct colors. It is important to ascertain what fiber the blanket is made from first and check the dye manufacturers' instructions before you begin to avoid disappointing results.

YOU WILL NEED:

an old blanket

cold water dye and recommended fixative

dyebath

velvet fabric measuring 54 in (137 cm) wide – for quantity measure length of blanket plus 16 in (40 cm)

1¼ in (3 cm) wide ribbon – for quantity measure length and width of blanket twice plus 14 in (35 cm)

needle and thread

96 in (240 cm) of 1½ in (4 cm) wide taffeta ribbon

pattern paper

pencil

ruler

1 Weigh the blanket and calculate the amount of dye required as instructed by the dye manufacturers. Wash the blanket thoroughly and leave it damp. The dyebath needs to be big enough so that the blanket will be fully immersed in the dye. Prepare the dye bath and dye the blanket following the manufacturer's instructions. When the blanket takes on the chosen color, remove it from the dye bath and rinse thoroughly until the water is clear. Gently squeeze out excess water and hang the blanket up to dry.

2 To make a pattern for the long side border, draw a front seam line the same length as the side measurement of the blanket on to pattern paper. Draw another line 11 in (28 cm) from and parallel to the front seam line for the back seam, with the fold line marked running midway between the lines. Make a mark 5½ in (14 cm) beyond both ends of the fold line and draw lines to join the ends of the front and back seam lines to these marks. Add ⅝ in (1.5 cm) to all edges for seam allowance. Make another pattern piece in the same way for the top and bottom border using the measurement of the width of the blanket. Cut out two of each border piece in velvet.

3 Pin and tack lengths of ribbon along the front of each border piece so that the bottom edge lies ½ in (1 cm) away from the seam line. Stitch in place close to both edges of the ribbon. Right sides facing, join a side border to the top border and the other side border to the bottom border, then join both sections together. Clip the seams and trim the corners and turn to right side. Press the mitered corners flat. With the right side of the border to the right side of the blanket, pin the front seam border edge to the blanket, tack and stitch all round. Trim the seam, turn the border to the right side and turning under the back seam allowance pin the back seam line to the back of the blanket and slip stitch in place.

70

4 To make the ribbon roses, cut the taffeta ribbon into four 24 in (60 cm) lengths. Take one of these lengths and start by folding one end of the ribbon lengthways. Then, keeping the selvedges underneath the flower, pleat and turn the ribbon around itself a few times to form the center. Secure at the base with a few stitches using a needle and thread. Begin to open out the ribbon and continue pleating, turning and stitching it at the base as the rose forms. Fold the end of the ribbon to hide it under the base and stitch in place. Stitch a ribbon rose in place at each corner of the blanket.

Patched Napkins

THESE NAPKINS MADE FROM FABRIC with a wonderfully eccentric pattern of bright red zinnias and stylized yellow and green leaves would brighten any table. This is a real example of how 'a little goes a long way'. Only a small piece of this floral furnishing fabric remained, but it provided the starting point for these designs and, with a little ingenuity, a set of four napkins was produced. Contrasting fabrics in cream, pink and red were used to highlight the vibrant colors of the zinnias and the leaves.

The overall effect is similar to log cabin patchwork, but rather than laboriously stitching small pieces together, squares of differing sizes were laid one on top of another. The napkins can be sewn by hand or by machine, and can be further embellished if you wish. Try adding small buttons to the corners or over-sew the seams with simple embroidery such as blanket stitch in a brightly colored cotton embroidery thread.

Cottage garden flowers – vibrant zinnias on the fabric and cheerful dahlias in the pale pink jug – provide the inspiration for this 1950s-inspired setting.

Patched Napkins

Each napkin measures
14 in (36 cm) square.

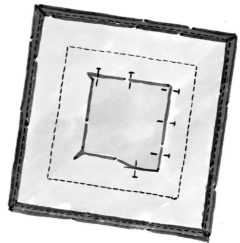

FOR 4 NAPKINS YOU
WILL NEED:

*36 in (90 cm) lightweight
linen measuring
54 in (137) cm wide*

*12 in (30 cm) patterned
linen measuring
54 in (137 cm) wide*

4 scraps of plain linen

sewing thread

pencil

pins

sewing machine

1 To make one napkin, cut out a
16 in (41 cm) square of lightweight linen.
Turn under and press a hem of ½ in (1 cm)
then ⅜ in (1.5 cm) on all four sides, making
double mitered corners as shown on page
78. Pin then stitch the hem in place. To make
the first patch, cut a 10½ in (26 cm) square
in patterned linen. Press under ⅜ in (1 cm)
on each side and single mitre the corners as
shown on page 78. Place the patch centrally
on the right side of the napkin, pin then
stitch close to the edges.

2 Turn the napkin to the wrong side and
draw a 5 in (13 cm) square centrally on
the back with pencil. Cut along the pencil
lines through the napkin fabric to remove
the square and leave the patch showing
through. Turn under ⅜ in (1 cm) on all four
sides, snipping with scissors into each corner
to just within the turning, pin then stitch
close to the turned edge.

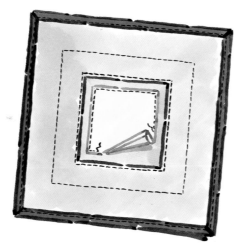

3 Cut out a 5 in (13 cm) square from a
scrap of plain linen for the second patch.
Turn under ½ in (1 cm) hems on all four
sides, making single mitered corners as
before, and pin it centrally to the wrong side
of the first patch on the back of the napkin.
Stitch it in place close to the edges.

4 Turn the napkin to the right side and
draw a 2½ in (6 cm) square in the middle
of the first patch with a pencil, then cut the
square away to leave the second patch
showing through. Turn under ½ in (1 cm) on
each side of the square, snipping the corners
as before. Pin in place, then stitch close to
the edges

Templates and Stitches

RUNNING STITCH The simplest of all embroidery stitches, this consists of short stitches going in and out of the fabric forming a broken line. Suitable for straight and curved lines.

BACK STITCH Forms an unbroken line. Take a long stitch underneath the fabric, bring the needle up then take it back and insert it through the fabric at the end of the last stitch.

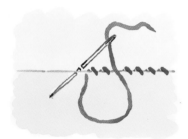

SLIP STITCH To join two pieces of fabric neatly, fold the top piece over and slide the needle through the fold and then back through the lower fabric, making small neat stitches.

BLANKET STITCH Useful for decorative hemming. Bring the thread through from the wrong side near the edge of the fabric, then move the needle to the side. Push it through the fabric again and down through the thread loop.

FLY STITCH An attractive embroidery stitch, this is made by taking a horizontal stitch, bringing the needle up in the middle, slightly lower down and over the thread, then taking a vertical stitch.

FEATHER STITCH Take a horizontal stitch, bring the needle up through the fabric again, slightly lower, and over the thread. Make another stitch to one side, then another to line up with the first to form a zig zag line.

DOUBLE FEATHER STITCH This is a variation on feather stitch, with two stitches done to one side and then another two to the other side, forming a more pronounced zigzag effect.

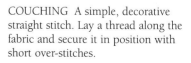

COUCHING A simple, decorative straight stitch. Lay a thread along the fabric and secure it in position with short over-stitches.

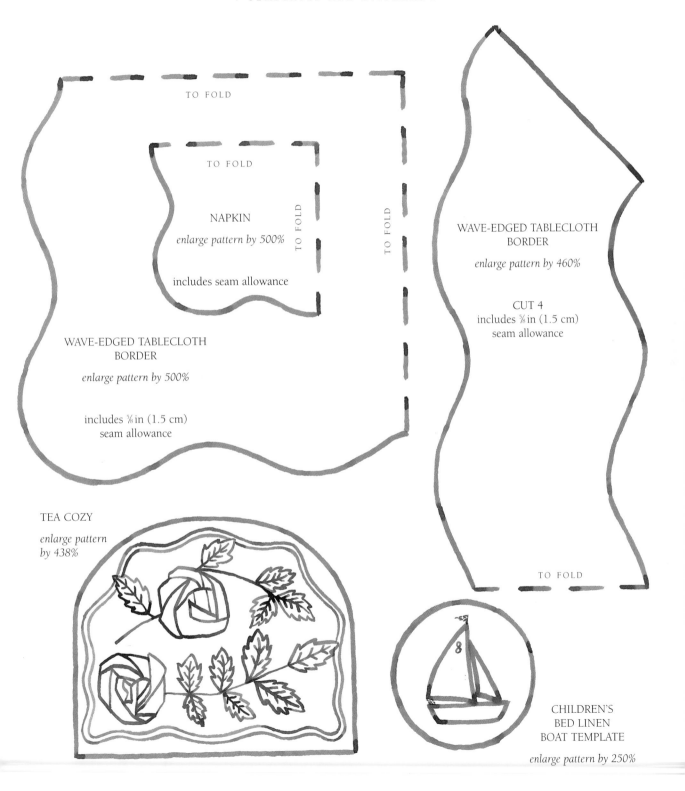

TO FOLD

TO FOLD

TO FOLD

TO FOLD

NAPKIN

enlarge pattern by 500%

includes seam allowance

WAVE-EDGED TABLECLOTH
BORDER

enlarge pattern by 500%

includes ⅝ in (1.5 cm)
seam allowance

WAVE-EDGED TABLECLOTH
BORDER

enlarge pattern by 460%

CUT 4
includes ⅝ in (1.5 cm)
seam allowance

TO FOLD

TEA COZY

*enlarge pattern
by 438%*

CHILDREN'S
BED LINEN
BOAT TEMPLATE

enlarge pattern by 250%

Single Mitre

Fold in a hem of equal depth on both sides of the fabric. Press in place, then unfold the hem. Turn the corner over diagonally and press. Carefully cut off the corner point, close to the pressed lines. Fold over the remaining corner fabric, fold in the two sides, press and stitch in place.

Double Mitre

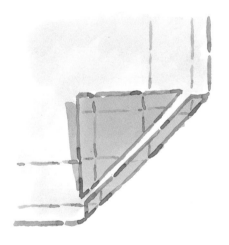

This is done in a similar way to the single mitre, but the sides are turned over twice. This means that the raw edges are hidden when the sides are hemmed.

Acknowledgements

The author would like to thank the following companies, shops and suppliers for their help and generosity in loaning items for photography.

Damask, The Iron Bed Company, Malabar, Pavilion Textiles, Sanderson, Sibona, Turquaz.

I would like to thank the following people who have contributed their time and special talents to this book. Emma Hardy whose assistance throughout has been invaluable and who made the pajamas, velvet-edged blankets and linen bags as well as helping to carry piles of linens and camera equipment to and fro; Alice Nicol, my mother, for the cross-stitch monograms and her constant support; Julia Sorrel for using her distinctive style to appliqué and embroider the quilt; Karen Spurgin for stitching the rose tea cozy and Isabel Stanley for designing and making the children's bed linen set.

Thanks also to the following people who kindly allowed us to use their homes as locations and settings for the photographs: John Morgan, Julie Hailey, Joe and Yvonne Hobbs from The Utility Rooms and Freddie Hair.

I would like to thank Cindy Richards and Kate Haxell from Collins & Brown for their support and encouragement throughout the project, Christine Wood for designing the pages so beautifully and Kate Simunek and Gillian Haslam for their essential contributions to this book.

For my nieces Emma, Anna and Pheobe

First published in the United States of America in 1998 by Trafalgar Square Publishing, North Pomfret, Vermont 05053

Printed and bound in China by Donnelly & Sons

First published in Great Britain in 1998 by Collins & Brown Limited

1 3 5 7 9 8 6 4 2

Library of Congress Catalog Card Number: 97-81205

ISBN 1-57076-115-9

Designer: Christine Wood
Photographer: Gloria Nicol

Reproduction by HBM Print

Index